INSTANT GUITAR

CHARLES SEGAL
COLLEEN SEGAL

Cover design and layout: Kayla Glovinski **Music printing**: Kevin O'Shaughnessy

© 1973 Segal's Publications, 58 Burg Street, Cape Town, South Africa
© 2010 Charles Segal Publications, 16 Grace Rd. Ste 1, Newton, MA 02459
All rights reserved.
ISBN: 1456495690
ISBN-13: 978-1456495695

ABOUT THE AUTHORS

Charles Segal has enjoyed a long and multi-faceted career in the music business in diverse roles as musician, composer, music publisher, producer, and teacher. His many prestigious awards include the equivalent of a Grammy - South African Record Industry (SARI) Award for Song of the Year for "My Children, My Wife" (in this book).

Charles is an amazing teacher. He was trained in mandolin and classical piano performance and composition and attained a teacher's Licentiate from the Trinity College of London. His "INSTANT" series of music tutor books helps guide aspiring musicians quickly and easily through the basics and his private students find themselves playing INSTANTLY at the first lesson.

Charles is the featured artist on over 500 albums. He has worked with great musicians, like Cy Coleman, Bill Evans, Bud Powell, Dan Hill and Arthur Prysock; he composes and plays "loops" for Hip-Hop artists and is a popular performer at Hollywood events in celebration of awards such as the Oscars, MTV Movie Awards, Teen and Kids Choice. Charles' work spans a myriad of cultures and styles, including Pop, Jazz, Classical, Contemporary, Film score, Ethnic, African, Relaxing and New Age music. He has produced albums with pop groups, traditional African groups, and also children's music for his own label and international record companies. See more at www.CharlesSegal.com.

Co-writer Colleen met Charles when she was a keyboardist and singer in the trendy pop group, The In-Set. She is a teacher and author, co-composer and producer of eight full-length musicals, short stories, speech tutors and the INSTANT Music tutor series.

Contact the authors through our website: www.CharlesSegal.com.
Hear some Charles Segal original songs on iTunes.

ABOUT THIS BOOK

INSTANT GUITAR is a quick introduction to playing the guitar and reading music.

We wrote **INSTANT GUITAR** because we know there's an **easier way for people to learn the GUITAR just for fun**. Let's face it: old-fashioned music lessons are confusing.

So, we sifted through our teaching experience to find the **bare minimum you need to get you started having fun playing your favorite songs, INSTANTLY.**

10 GREAT THINGS ABOUT INSTANT GUITAR:

(1)   **INSTANT GUITAR** gets right to the heart of what you need to know to play.

(2)   **INSTANT GUITAR** lets you play at the very first lesson.

(3)   **INSTANT GUITAR** gives you choices: learn to READ MUSIC INSTANTLY, or go straight to page 30 and learn to play INSTANT CHORDS so you can play along while you sing.

(4)   **INSTANT GUITAR** teaches you to tap the rhythm before learning to read music.

(5)   **INSTANT GUITAR** makes the whole process of **reading music painless**, with our **easy, step-by-step** course that lets you in on the **insider tricks**.

(6)   **INSTANT GUITAR** is bursting with **popular songs – all in the same key!**

(7)   **INSTANT GUITAR** gives you **INSTANT CHORD CHARTS** so you can easily play other songs that aren't in this book.

(8)   The main thing about **INSTANT GUITAR** is that it allows you to have fun **playing right away**, while teaching you **only what you absolutely need to know** to play.

(9)   **INSTANT GUITAR** is a springboard to other books in the INSTANT Series, like **Instant Guitar II, Instant Keyboard, Instant Songwriting** and more.

(10)   The **best thing** about **INSTANT GUITAR** is: you can **contact us any time with any questions** by going to our **website: www.CharlesSegal.com**

Have fun!

Sincerely,

Charles Segal and Colleen Segal

CONTENTS

THE GUITAR

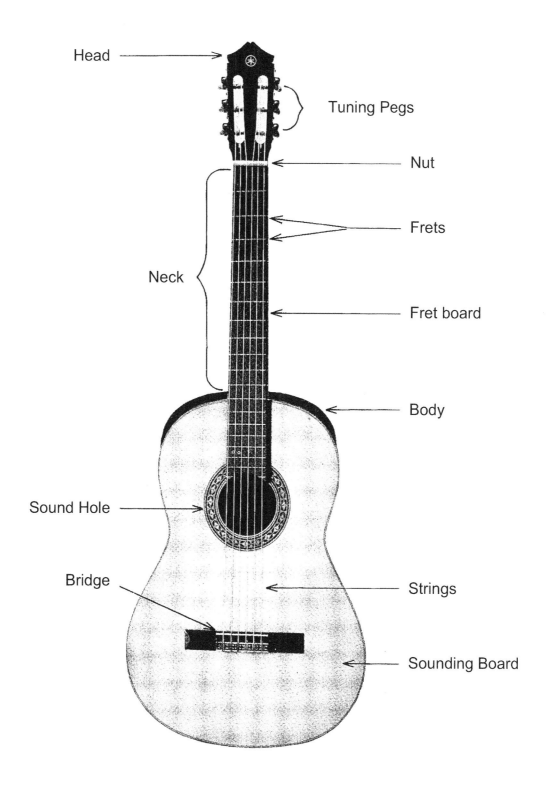

Head

Tuning Pegs

Nut

Frets

Neck

Fret board

Body

Sound Hole

Strings

Bridge

Sounding Board

THE RIGHT HAND

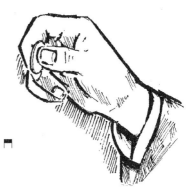

The **PICK** is held firmly between the thumb and first finger.

Keep your wrist relaxed.

Pick tunes with a **downward** motion indicated by this sign ⊓

An **upward** motion is indicated by this sign ∨

START PLAYING INSTANTLY:

Exercise #1

Using your pick, play the open strings one at a time with a downward motion, starting with the top string and making sure that you pick only that string and not its neighbor.

Play each string 4 times before moving down to play the next string.

When you reach the bottom string, play it again 4 times and then go upwards to the next string, playing that 4 times, until you are back at the top string.

Exercise #2

Now jump around and play the strings in a different order. For example, play String 6, then 4, then 2, then 5, then 1, then 3.

Have fun playing whichever strings you want to, in any order, repeating the sounds once, twice, three or four times.

This is your very first tune – enjoy it!

THE LEFT HAND

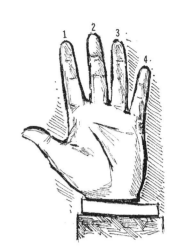

The fingers of the left hand are numbered 1, 2, 3, 4 starting at the index finger.

Fingers 1 – 4 press the strings onto the fingerboard to form notes or chords.

The thumb is positioned behind the second fret to act as counter pressure for the fingers pressing the strings.

Keep your wrist away from the fingerboard when playing. This puts your fingers in a better position to play the notes.

The strings must be pressed firmly by the fingers, without touching a neighboring string. To play a particular note, place your fingers firmly on the strings directly behind the frets and the sound the string with the pick in your right hand.

START PLAYING INSTANTLY:

Exercise #1

Have fun playing around with different strings, pressing any frets until you can play a good, round sound each time.

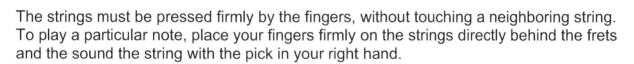

When you sound a note without pressing a fret on that string, you have played an "open string".

Exercise #2

Once you feel confident playing single strings, try playing two strings at the same time.

Now try adding two different frets to see how many different sounds you can make.

Have fun experimenting by playing any sounds you like.

THE FRET BOARD

This is a diagram to show you where to place the fingers of your left hand on the fret board. You will see it used later in the book to demonstrate chords.

The vertical lines are the strings.

The horizontal lines are the frets.

The numbers above are the numbers of the strings, numbered 1 – 6, starting with lowest, thinnest string.

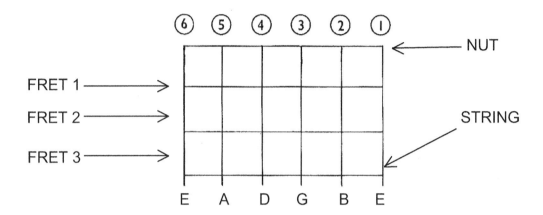

TUNING THE GUITAR

Guitar strings are tuned by tightening or loosening them, using the six tuning pegs at the head of the guitar. Guitar strings can be tuned to a variety of different pitches. In this book you will use STANDARD TUNING.

Tightening a string raises the pitch of a note.

Loosening a string lowers the pitch of a note.

Try it: pick a string with your right hand while you gently and slowly turn the tuning peg with your left hand. Notice how the pitch becomes higher or lower depending on which way you turn the tuning peg.

Caution: try this slowly and carefully and do not over-tighten as too much tension could cause a string to snap.

PIANO METHOD

The six open strings of the guitar should match the pitches of the six notes shown in the diagram of the piano keyboard. Note that 5 of the strings are below "Middle C".

Tune the strings one at a time, playing the piano note and then picking the open string.

Turn each tuning peg slowly and gently until the pitch made by the string matches the pitch played on the piano.

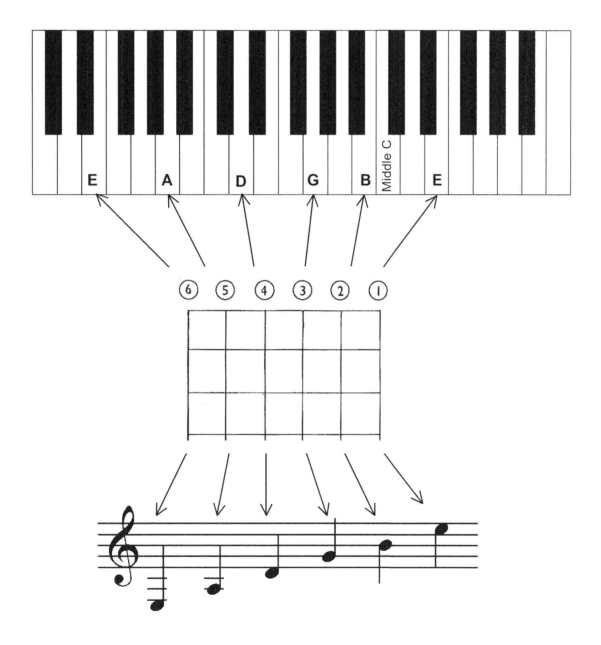

RELATIVE TUNING

1. Tune the 6th string to E using either the piano method listed above or by using an electronic tuner if a piano is not available.

2. Place your finger behind the 5th fret on the 6th string; this pitch is A.

3. Play the 6th and 5th strings together and, using the tuning peg, adjust the pitch of the 5th string up or down until it matches the pitch created by the depressed 6th string. When the two pitches match perfectly, the 5th string is "in tune."

4. Press the 5th string at the 5th fret and tune the open 4th string to that pitch.

5. Press the 4th string at the 5th fret and tune the open 3rd string to that pitch.

6. Press the 3rd string at the 4th fret and tune the open 2nd string to that pitch.

7. Press the 2nd string and the 5th fret and tune the open 1st string to that pitch.

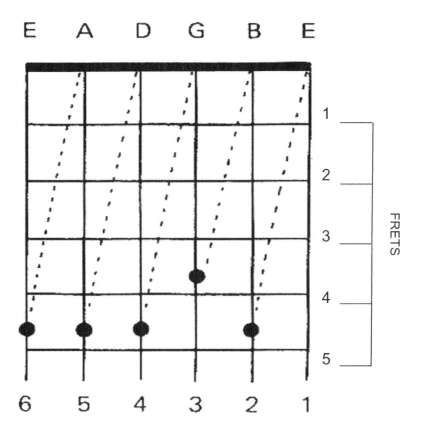

HOW TO READ MUSIC

Music is written as NOTES on a STAFF, which has FIVE LINES and FOUR SPACES.

STAFF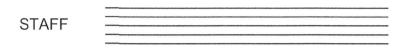

At the beginning of each staff is a CLEF.

All guitar music is written in the TREBLE CLEF.

TREBLE
CLEF ⟶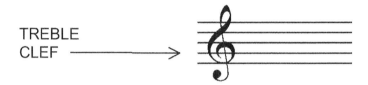

The position of a note placed on the staff, high or low, determines its pitch.

Notes may be placed…

ON the staff   **BELOW** the staff   **ABOVE** the staff

Notes placed below or above the staff use ledger lines to show their pitch.

Notes take the names of the lines or spaces they occupy on the Staff.

The names of music notes are the first seven letters of the Alphabet: A B C D E F G.
Below is the musical alphabet written on the staff. The seven letters repeat after "G".

You will notice that going from one note to the next note, higher or lower on the scale, music notes are written from a LINE to the NEXT SPACE, to the NEXT LINE and so on.

To make reading music easier, memorize the line notes and space notes below.

LINE NOTES: **E G B D F** (**E**very **G**ood **B**oy **D**oes **F**ine)

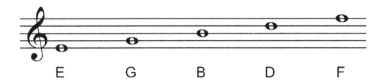

E   G   B   D   F

SPACE NOTES: **F A C E** (These space letters spell "face")

F   A   C   E

MATCHING WRITTEN MUSIC TO THE GUITAR

On the pages that follow you will see how written music relates to playing the guitar. The diagrams show you exactly which strings to play, whether the string is played open or if a fret is pressed, and which finger to use.

In your very first exercise in reading and playing notes, you will be playing three notes on the first string – the notes are right next to each other in the scale: E, F and G.

On the guitar you will play an open first string for E, then press down the 1st and the 3rd frets of the first string for F and G.

Be aware if a note moves upwards or downwards on the staff.

In the first line of Exercise 1 you play SPACE notes (E) and go up to LINE notes (F) and then back down to SPACE NOTES (E) again.

Watch out for the jump in line 2 from a SPACE (G) down to the next SPACE (E).

NOTES ON THE FIRST STRING – E

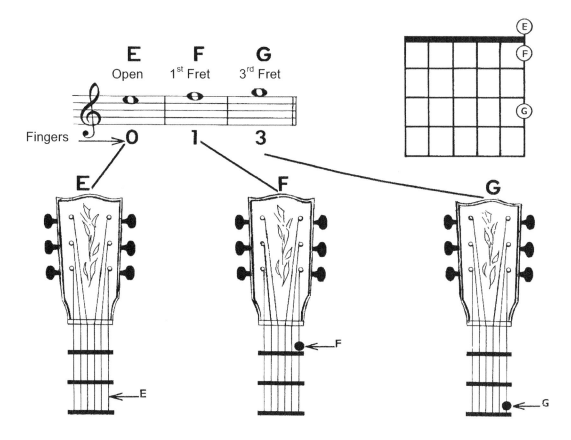

Play the following exercises slowly and evenly using only the down stroke. Make sure you play each note written and that each sound you make is clear and full. Play each exercise several times over until you feel confident.

9

INSTANT TIMING

When you play songs that you already know, you play the timing of the notes from memory, so you don't have to concentrate on reading note values. But it is useful to know something about musical timing for reasons that will become obvious as you proceed in your musical education.

THE RHYTHM OR THE BEAT

Wherever there is music, you will see people nodding their heads, tapping their feet or clapping out the beat, even if they don't know the tune or the lyrics. That is because **rhythm is at the very root of all music**. **The rhythm or beat remains steady and at the same speed throughout a song.** When you listen to music, most won't notice a wrong note here or there, but everyone notices when the rhythm is off. **The INSTANT method will help you keep a steady rhythm in your playing.**

CONNECTING TO THE RHYTHM

Rhythm is innate in every human being. From the steady beating of our heart to the rhythm of our walking; whether talking, performing or dancing, everyone has rhythm. To connect to the beat in music, the trick is to harness our instinctive rhythm and use it to enhance our playing.

In the pages that follow you will learn how to read musical timing in written notes. But first you should learn the INSTANT way to keep in time and on beat.

BEAT TAPPING

Whenever you listen to, or sing, or play music, you should tap your foot or nod your head to keep the beat. You may already do this naturally, but if you don't, then **begin right away**.

STEP 1: Listen to or think of a song you like. Find the beat. The beat is not the melody, but that strong 1 - 2 - 3 - 4 pulse of the bass drum in a band.

STEP 2: Tap out the beat of the song with your foot (or by nodding your head) and do not stop until the song is over.

STEP 3: Remember to tap the beat every time you listen to or play music.

HOW TO COUNT IN MUSIC

Counting and beat tapping happen simultaneously and must always be even.

In music, the beat **must always be steady**, so play more slowly if you are unsure of the notes and don't pause when you are looking for a melody note or a chord.

It is better to find the melody or chord notes first and practice the pattern of the tune or chord changes until you know them well – then add the time values and the beat.

Counting a note's value starts from the moment you sound the note.
You pick the string, count "one" and tap your foot at the same time.
Sustain the note for the entire amount of its time value.

Now go back and play the exercises from Notes on the First String. Each of the notes in Exercises 1 - 4 is worth **one beat**.

When you play the notes give **one count and one beat tap for each note.**

Exercise #1

Notice the pattern of four notes followed by a vertical line (**BAR LINE**). The space between the bar-lines is called a "**BAR**" or "**MEASURE**". At the end of the exercise, there is a **DOUBLE BAR LINE**. This exercise has **four beats in a bar**.

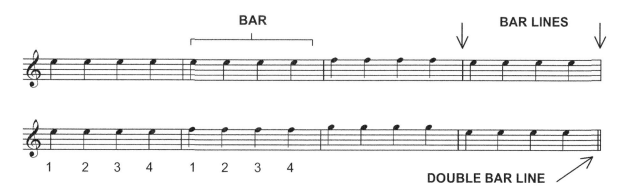

Before playing the notes, look at the music and read the notes, counting steadily and slowly one count for each note: "**1 – 2 – 3 – 4 – 1 – 2 – 3 – 4**"

Try again: This time, tap your foot on each count as you read the notes.

Notice that Exercise #1 consists of two lines. When you get to the end of line one, continue to line two without stopping the beat until the double bar line at the end.

Once you can keep a steady beat, pick out the notes on your guitar, slowly and steadily, counting and tapping the beat as you play. **Repeat this method for the rest of the exercises on the First String.**

NOTE VALUES

Note values are part of the rhythm of a song.

Sing any song and you will notice that, while the steady beat is always the same, some melody notes are short or fast and other notes are held for longer.

In written music the **shape of a note denotes its time value.**

So, a note placed on the staff not only tells you WHERE to play it on the Guitar, but it also indicates the LENGTH OF TIME it must be held.

Below is a diagram giving you an overview **of some musical notes, their time values and their names:**

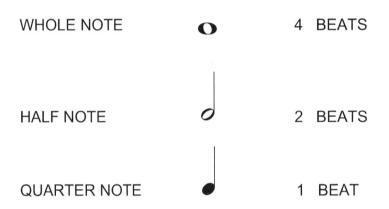

WHOLE NOTE		4 BEATS
HALF NOTE		2 BEATS
QUARTER NOTE		1 BEAT

Exercise #1 *"Whole Note Serenade"*

1 2 3 4   1 2 3 4

Pick the note and tap your foot on the count of "1"

The sound continues (without you playing it again) while you **tap your foot and count out "2 – 3 – 4".** The counts are written under the staff.

Until you can find the notes of a tune easily, to practice keeping the counts and beats in time, you can clap instead of playing the notes while you tap and count.

Once you feel confident that you can find the notes and add the counting, you can slowly and steadily, count, tap and pick the notes of the tune from beginning to end without stopping.

TIP: give yourself four steady counts and foot taps before you begin to play any melody

Exercise #2 *"Half Note March"*

1   2   3   4   1   2   3   4

How to play and count Half Notes:

Pick the note and tap your foot on the count of "1"

The sound continues (without you playing it again) while you **tap your foot and count out "2"**

On the count of **"3"** you will play the next note in the tune and tap your foot.

The sound continues (without you playing it again) while you **tap your foot and count out "4"**

Try counting the half notes above, remembering to keep a steady beat with your foot tapping.

Clap or play the same line, tapping your foot on every count (even when you are not clapping or picking a note).

Exercise #3 *"Tuneful Quarter Note"*

1   2   3   4   1   2   3   4

How to play and count Quarter Notes:

You've played in Quarter Notes before – on the First String.

Keep an even beat with your foot and give one count for each quarter note.
You will be counting: **"1 – 2 – 3 – 4"** as you play the 4 notes in each bar.

Clap or play the quarter notes, counting aloud and tapping your foot.

TIME SIGNATURES

You have already seen that BAR-LINES divide music into segments of time called BARS.

The TIME SIGNATURE found just after the TREBLE CLEF at the beginning of a song establishes the RHYTHM (or METER) of a song.

The top number indicates the number of beats in each measure.

4 BEATS PER MEASURE.

QUARTER NOTE (♩) GETS ONE BEAT.

The bottom number indicates which note value will receive one beat.

The time signature $\frac{4}{4}$ ("four, four") may also be written as **C** ("Common Time").

Below is a different Time Signature.

Can you figure out what it means?

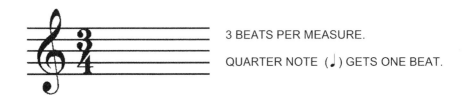

3 BEATS PER MEASURE.

QUARTER NOTE (♩) GETS ONE BEAT.

Your counts in a song in 3/4 time are: **"1 – 2 – 3 – 1 – 2 – 3"**

Look at the different Time Signatures in this book and see if you can count the beats.

NOTES ON THE SECOND STRING – B

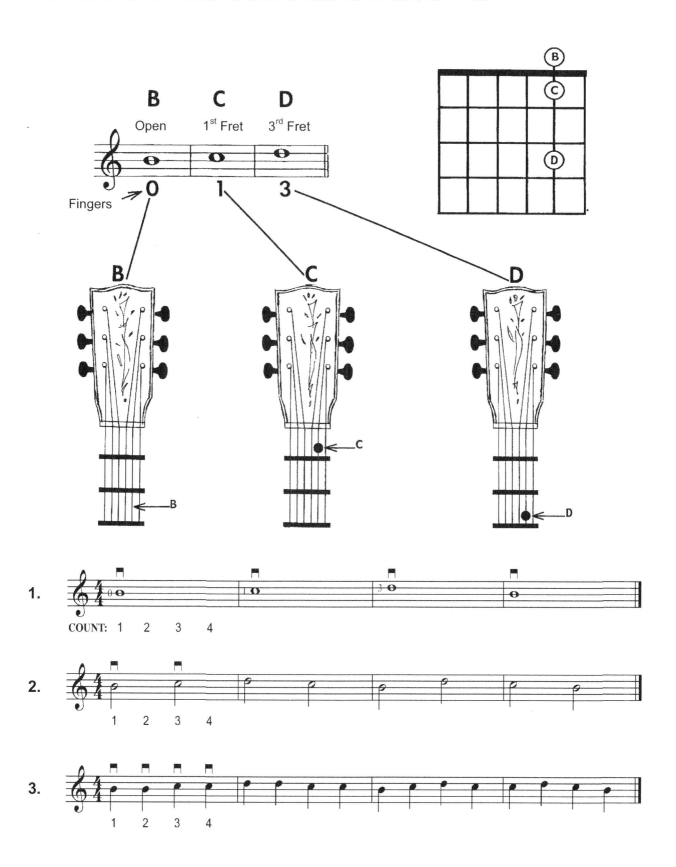

15

A NEW NOTE VALUE – DOTTED NOTES

A dot placed after any note increases the value of that note by one-half its original value. See the examples below. Even though you may rarely see some of these values, they will help you understand the concept:

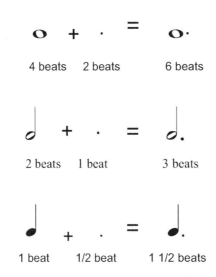

Exercise #1 *"Waltz of the Dotted Half Note"*

Notice the Time Signature at the beginning of this melody is 3/4 time, indicating that there are **3 BEATS in each bar**.

Play this tune, picking the notes on the count of "1" and counting "2 – 3" before playing the next note on the count of "1".

Exercise #2 *"Mixture"*

This is a mixture of Whole Notes, Half Notes, Dotted Half Notes and Quarter Notes. Notice the Time Signature indicates that there are **4 BEATS in each bar**. Practice tapping, counting and playing these notes.

Exercise #3: *"Two String Waltz"*

This is the first time you will be playing a melody on two different strings, so practice getting your fingers coordinated to switch from one string to another.

The tune starts on the First String and then, (in the 5th and 6th Bars and the last 3 Bars of the song) there are notes that are played on the Second String. Can you see them?

This melody is in 3/4 time – with **3 BEATS in a BAR**.

First find the notes and practice the tune until you are confident.

Next, work on the timing, counting and clapping out the notes you're going to play.

Then slowly play the tune with a steady beat, without any pauses to find the notes.

"TWO STRING WALTZ"

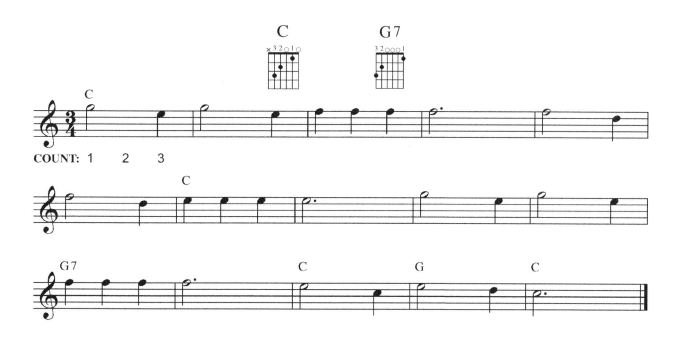

Notice that there are fingerboard diagrams above the song. The letters ("C" and "G") also appear above the staff at various points in the song. These are Chord Symbols that you can use later for playing Chords along with the melody. For now you can ignore them.

Exercise #4:

These well-known songs are played on the First and Second Strings. Learn the notes, add the counts, then play the whole song with a steady beat and no pauses until the end.

"JINGLE BELLS"

"MOLLY MALONE"

"LIGHTLY ROW"

Light - ly row, light - ly row, o'er the glas - sy waves we go.

Smooth - ly glide, smooth - ly glide, on the si - lent tide.

Let the winds and wa - ters be, ming - led with our mel - o - dy.

Sing and float, sing and float, in our lit - tle boat.

"DRINK TO ME ONLY WITH THINE EYES"

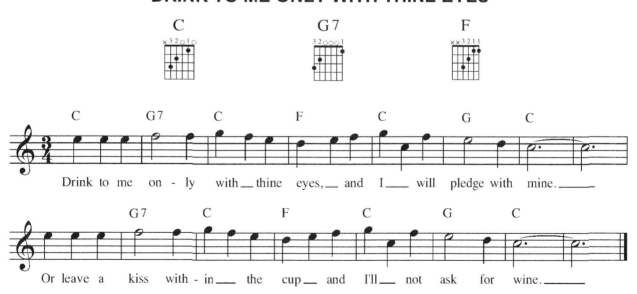

Drink to me on - ly with __ thine eyes, __ and I __ will pledge with mine. ____

Or leave a kiss with - in __ the cup __ and I'll __ not ask for wine. ____

TIED NOTES

Notice in the last two bars of each line of the previous song, there is a curved line between two C notes. This is a TIE, which joins **two notes of the same pitch.**
The first note is picked and **sounded for the time duration of both notes.**
The **second note of the Tie is not picked**, but is still counted.

Exercise #1

play   *hold*   *play*   *hold*   *play*   *hold*   *play*   *hold*

Exercise #2

Exercise #3

Go back and play "Drink to Me Only With Thine Eyes", playing and counting the TIED NOTES correctly and then play Beautiful Brown Eyes".

"BEAUTIFUL BROWN EYES"

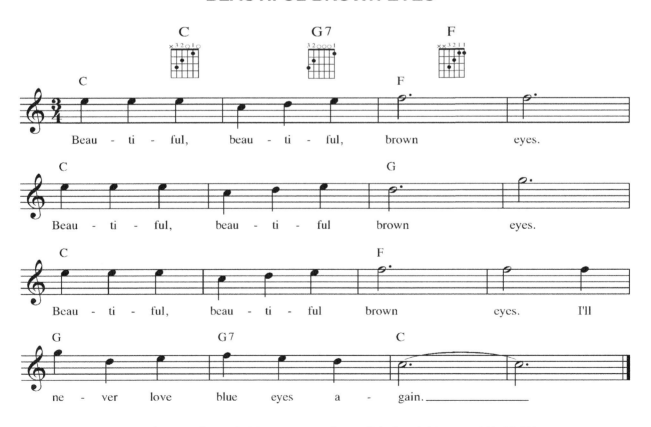

NOTES ON THE THIRD STRING – G

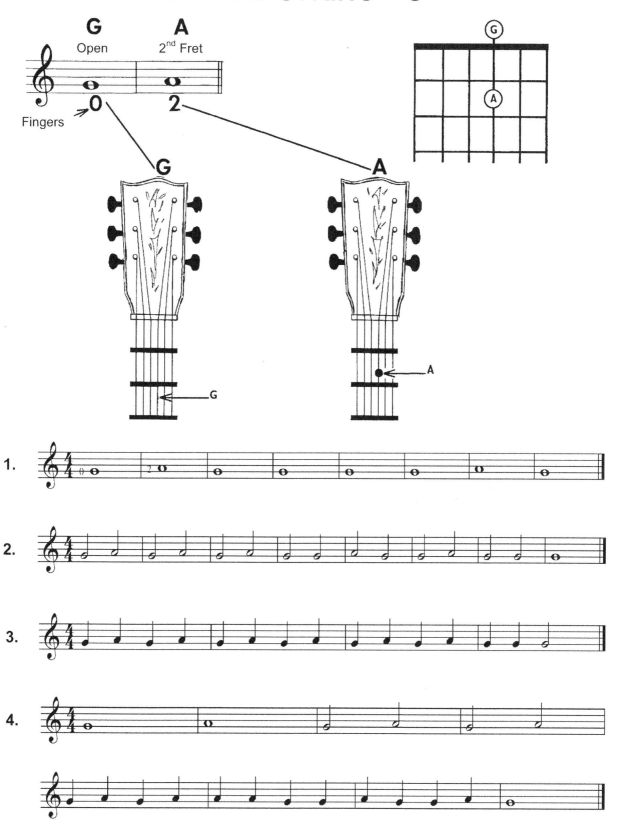

NOTES ON THE FOURTH STRING – D

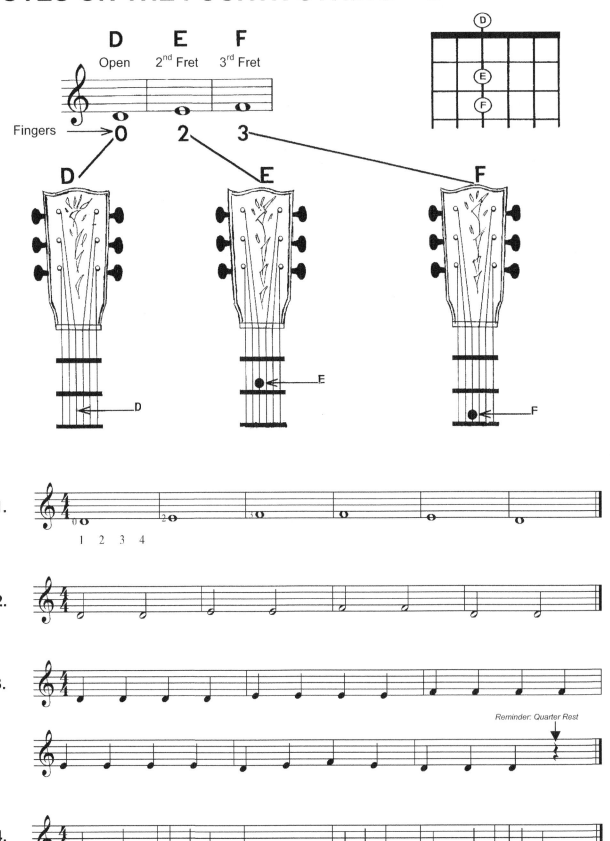

NOTES ON THE FIFTH STRING – A

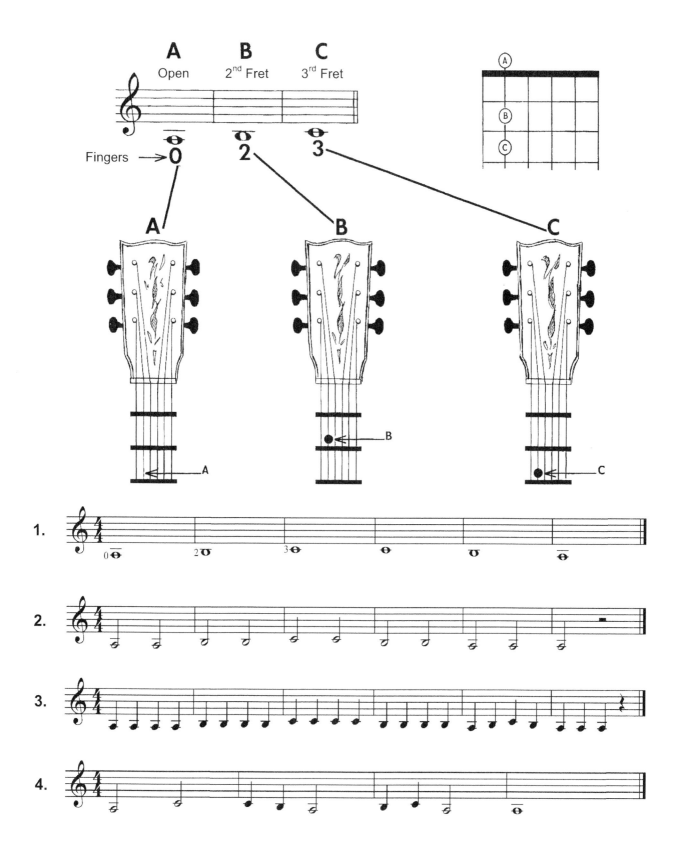

"SONG OF THE VOLGA BOATMAN"

"LONDON BRIDGE"

Lon - don bridge is fall - ing down, fall - ing down, fall - ing down.

Lon - don bridge is fall - ing down my fair La - dy.

"YANKEE DOODLE"

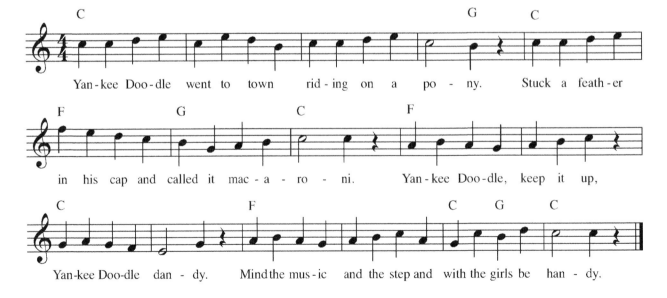

Yan - kee Doo - dle went to town rid - ing on a po - ny. Stuck a feath - er

in his cap and called it mac - a - ro - ni. Yan - kee Doo - dle, keep it up,

Yan - kee Doo - dle dan - dy. Mind the mus - ic and the step and with the girls be han - dy.

RESTS

Did you notice those squiggly signs in "Yankee Doodle"? (See it in the 4th bar – and more?) These are RESTS – signs used to designate a period of **silence.** RESTS have the same durations as the notes to which they correspond.

Here are examples of the RESTS on the staff in 4/4 time. The counts are written in.

The Whole and the Half Rests look similar, but the 4-count rest is higher in the space than the 2-count rest. (To remember, use a balloon analogy: more air (value) = floats higher).

Practice counting and playing the exercises below.

Exercise #1

Exercise #2

Exercise #3

NOTES ON THE SIXTH STRING – E

Here are even more Ledger Lines. Count the alphabet backwards from the first ledger line, C, down to below the third ledger line and you'll find E - the first note on the open Sixth string.

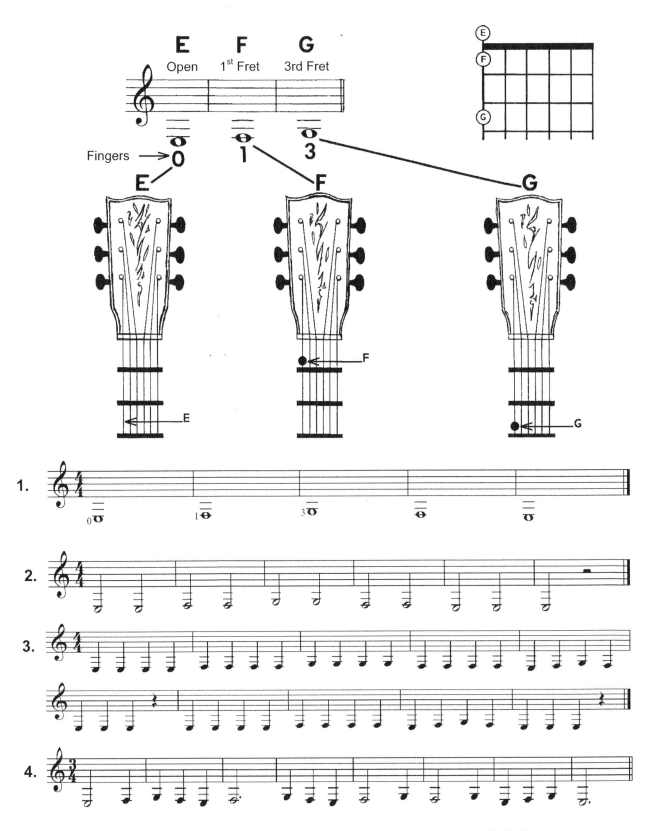

Exercise #3

Play this next song with notes on four strings.
First find the correct notes, before we talk about the timing.

"SHE'LL BE COMING 'ROUND THE MOUNTAIN"

PICK-UP NOTES

Not all music starts on the first beat. A PICK-UP is a lead-in to the first full bar of music. In the example below you will see that there are only 2 beats in the first bar and the last bar, but there is a 4/4 time signature. This song starts on the last 2 beats of the bar, so the count starts on "3 – 4" and ends in the last bar on "1 – 2". Because the beat in music has to be balanced, **when a pick-up is used in the first bar of a song, the last bar will be short the exact same number of beats** missing from the first bar.

Exercise #1

To count the pick-up notes in this exercise first establish a steady beat by counting a bar of 4/4 aloud. This is often referred to as a "bar of nothing". The next four counts will be the pick-up bar. Beats **3** and **4** are the pick-up notes that are played.
Here is a count chart to help you:

"1 2 3 4 | 1 2 **3** **4**"
(silent count) | *(silent)* **play play**

Exercise #2

Begin this exercise in the same way as Exercise #1 - by counting aloud a bar of time, keeping in mind that there are only 3 beats in a bar.

"1   2   3 | 1   2   **3**"
(silent count) | *(silent)* **play**

Exercise #3

Go back and play "She'll Be Coming 'Round the Mountain". This time count out the timing, noticing the pick-up notes, tied notes and rests.

INSTANT CHORDS

Up to now you have been playing SINGLE MELODY NOTES, picking the strings one at a time. In CHORDS you play SEVERAL NOTES TOGETHER. This takes a little practice.
Let's start with just two strings played together – the First and Second strings.

Exercise #1

Notice that there are TWO NOTES WRITTEN ON THE SAME STEM.
These notes are played simultaneously, as one.

Notes played singly on the First and Second strings in the first bar are combined and played together in the next bar.

Now practice the next two songs, also with two notes played together.

Exercise #2

"THE SWING"

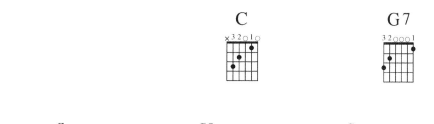

Exercise #3

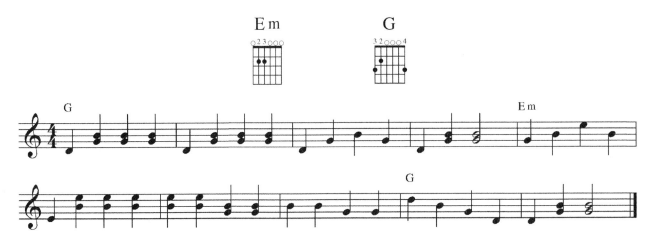

"SKIPPING TUNE"

A **MELODY** is a succession of **single notes**.

A **CHORD is a combination of** (usually 3) **notes sounded together.**

NOTES IN A MELODY   SAME NOTES AS A CHORD

Exercise #4

Practice this melody with single notes and then three-noted chords. Play carefully, making sure you can hear the difference between the single notes and the chord notes.

"CHORD WALTZ"

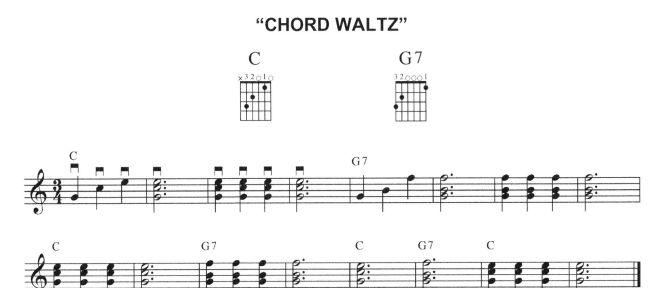

CHORD SYMBOLS AND DIAGRAMS

Looking back you'll notice that some of the melodies in this book have letters above the staff and others have letters and Fret Board diagrams. These are CHORD SYMBOLS and CHORD DIAGRAMS to help you play the right chord notes that go along with the melody.

You already know that a CHORD is 3 (or more) notes played together.
The CHORD SYMBOL identifies which chord is to be played.
The CHORD DIAGRAM **has all the information you need to play the chord:**
The left hand finger numbers to press the strings
The position on the fret board to be to be pressed
The strings that have to be picked.

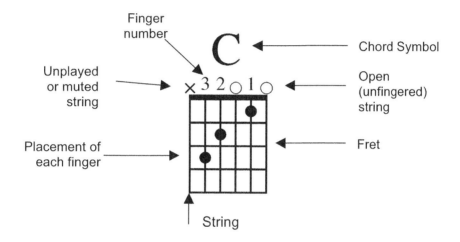

Practice playing the C Chord pictured in the diagram above.

Press 3 strings – the 2nd, 4th and 5th strings – with fingers 1, 2 and 3, and, leaving out the top, 6th string, you strum 5 strings with one downward motion of your pick. Keep strumming the C Chord over and over with a steady beat counting "1 – 2 – 3 – 4" as you play, until you feel confident and the sound of the chord has a full, rich tone.

Now play the G7 Chord.

Once you feel confident that your G7 chord has a good rich tone when you play it, practice strumming it for two bars counting "1 – 2 – 3 – 4" with a downward steady strum on each beat.

CHANGING CHORDS AND RHYTHMIC NOTATION

There is usually more than one chord in a song, so you should practice changing chords.

Play a C chord, then a G7 chord and back to a C chord again.
Do this several times until you can make smooth transitions without pausing.
Then try playing C several times on a steady beat, changing to G7 without stopping.
Remember to maintain a steady rhythm and keep chord transitions smooth.
Start slowly and gradually increase speed as you become comfortable with the changes.

RHYTHMIC NOTATION

You will notice that the quarter notes on the staff below look different.
This is because they are only indicating rhythm and not pitch.
This is called RHYTHMIC NOTATION.
Rhythmic notation is used to show when to strum a chord.

Exercise #1

The Chord Symbols above the bar show you which chord to strum and the Rhythmic Notation shows you the beats to strum.
In the exercise below you will strum on each of the 4 beats in a bar.
Strum C for 2 bars, followed by G7 for 2 bars.

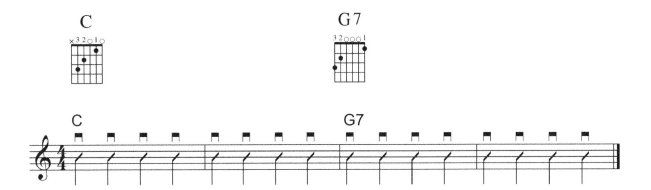

Exercise #2

There are 3 beats in a bar in this exercise, so you will strum C for 3 beats and G7 for 3 beats and then repeat the pattern.

Remember to **strum slowly without pausing the rhythm to change chords**.

Exercise #3

Find the songs in this book that have the C and G7 chords, like "London Bridge", "Molly Malone", "Lightly Row", and "The Swing". Practice strumming the chords.

A NEW CHORD - F

Exercise #4

F chords often appear in songs that have C and G7 chords. Practice transitioning between these three chords.

A NEW CHORD – G

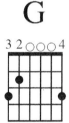

G7 and G are not the same chord, although they can often be interchangeable and sound similar.
Practice playing the G chord in the following song.

Exercise #5

"TWINKLE TWINKLE"

Exercise #6

Find all the songs with C, F, G and G7 chords. Practice strumming the chords.

A NEW TIME SIGNATURE – 2/4

Did you notice the new Time Signature in "Twinkle Twinkle"?

The 2/4 numbers tell you that each bar has two quarter note beats.

For each bar you will count: "1 – 2"

Try it.

1   2   1   2   1   2   1   2   1   2

CONGRATULATIONS!

You are now well on your way to becoming a guitar player!

BONUS SECTION

In the next section of the book you will find very helpful
tools to increase your understanding of music.
These tools include more musical signs,
more about timing and time-signatures,
chord charts, strumming patterns and lots of additional
songs to practice,
and much, much more!

REPEAT SIGNS AND ENDINGS

To save writing a melody that needs to be repeated, we use REPEAT SIGNS.
A Repeat Sign looks like this:

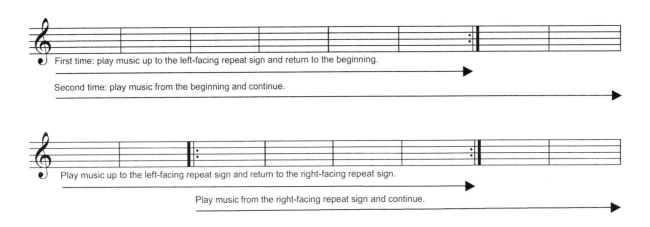

When two endings are needed (one to lead back to a repeated verse or chorus and one to end the song) we use FIRST and SECOND TIME BARS.
The FIRST TIME, play the bracketed section marked "1", and repeat the melody either from the beginning or from the inward-facing repeat sign:

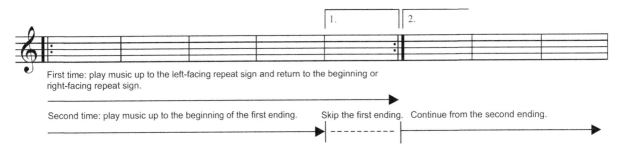

The SECOND TIME, leave out everything under the first time bracket and play the melody under the second time bracket, marked "2" until the end.

The next two songs have examples of Repeats and First and Second Time Bars.

"ROW, ROW, ROW YOUR BOAT"

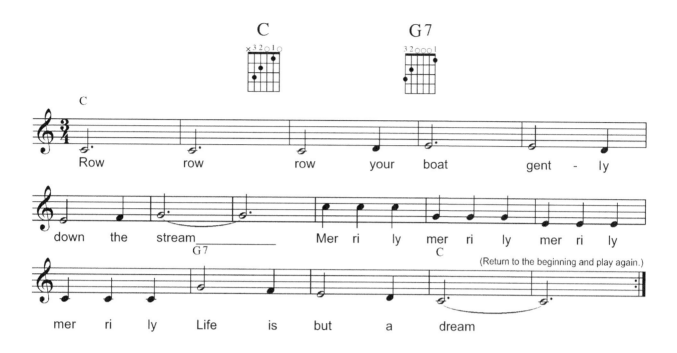

"CHOPSTICKS"

ACCIDENTALS – Sharps, Flats and Naturals

An ACCIDENTAL is a symbol placed before a note in order to raise it, lower it, or return it to its normal pitch. Accidentals affect only the pitches to which they are assigned and remain in effect throughout the same bar. The bar line will cancel any accidental.

When you see a SHARP ♯ in front of a note, play the NEXT FRET HIGHER

When you see a FLAT ♭ in front of a note, play the NEXT FRET LOWER

A NATURAL ♮ cancels a previous Accidental

Here's the more advanced version:
The distance between pitches is measured in SEMITONES and WHOLE TONES (or HALF-STEPS and WHOLE-STEPS).
On the guitar, **the distance between one fret and the next fret in either direction is called one Semitone.**
The distance between a fret and **two frets in either direction is called a Whole Tone.**
A SHARP raises a note by one fret (or semitone) and a FLAT lowers a note by one fret.

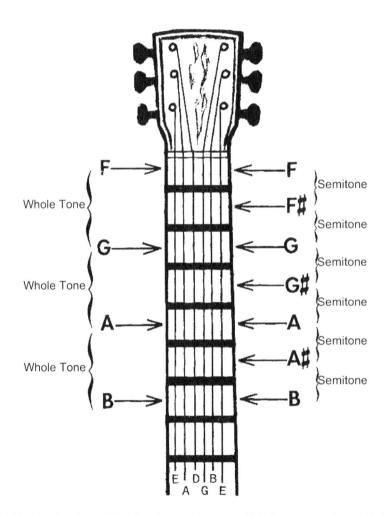

Exercise #1: Playing Sharps

Play these notes as written, remembering that a sharp tells you to play the **next fret higher.**

String Number

Exercise #2: Playing Flats

Play the **next fret lower** if the note is fingered.
If the note is an **open string, play the fourth fret of the next lower string.**

The exception is the open B string: the B-Flat is played on the third string, third fret.

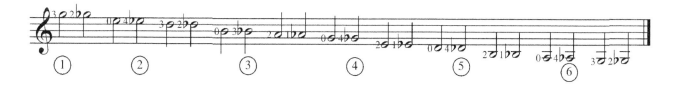

Exercise #3: Playing Naturals

Remember a natural **cancels a previous sharp or flat.**

Exercise #4: Mixture

The following example contains all of the Accidentals described above. Remember to pay particular attention to the flats in this example, as it may be necessary to play those notes on the next lower string.

KEY SIGNATURES

A sharp or flat appearing at the beginning of a line of music, immediately after the Treble Clef, is called a KEY SIGNATURE. Sharps or flats in a key signature affect every note of that name in the song. For example, a sharp in the Key Signature on the "F" line means that EVERY "F" in the song must be played as an "F-Sharp" UNLESS a natural appears before a particular "F" note.

The Key Signature of following song tells us that the song is in the key of G.

"MY BONNIE LIES OVER THE OCEAN"

EIGHTH NOTES

There are TWO EIGHTH NOTES to every Quarter Note.

Eighth notes may be written individually:

Multiple eighth notes may be BEAMED together:

An EIGHTH NOTE REST is written like this: ♪

Eighth notes are counted as follows: **"1 and 2 and 3 and 4 and"** or "1 + 2 + 3 + 4 +"

Exercise #1

Play the eighth notes below. To make these faster notes easier to pick, the first eighth note is played with a DOWN stroke and the second with an UP stroke. The "and" count and the up strokes both occur on the second half of each beat. Remember to find the notes before you add the counting. Then play with a steady beat and no stops.

"12 BAR BLUES"

The following song features a pick-up. Notice the key signature at the beginning of this song. It means that every F note in the song must be played as an F#.

"OH! SUSANNA"

I came from Al - a - ba - a wid my ban - jo on my knee, I'm

g'wan to Lou - si - an - a, My true love for to see. It

rain'd all night the day I left, the wea - ther it was dry, The

sun so hot I froze to death; Su - san - na, don't you cry.

Oh! Su - san - na, oh, don't you cry for me, I've

come from Al - a - ba - ma wid my ban - jo on my knee.

This song won a South African Grammy (SARI) for the **best song-of-the-year!**

"THE STAR SPANGLED BANNER"

6/8 TIME SIGNATURE

TIME SIGNATURE FORMULA:

The **top number indicates how many beats** in each bar.
The **bottom number denotes what kind of beats** they are.

6   6 BEATS IN A BAR
8   EIGHTH NOTE GETS ONE BEAT

COUNTING IN EIGHTH NOTES

In 4/4 time we counted 1 2 3 4 for each quarter note beat.

$$\frac{4}{4}$$ 1 2 3 4 | 1 2 3 4 | 1 2 3 4 | 1 2 3 4 ‖

In 6/8 time the **count is in eighth notes: 1 2 3 4 5 6**

$$\frac{6}{8}$$ 1 2 3 4 5 6 | 1 2 3 4 5 6 | 1 2 3 4 5 6 ‖

You have to think of the note values differently:

♪   =   1 beat

♩   =   2 beats

♩. =   3 beats

Here is an example of counting 3 bars with a 6/8 time signature:

1   2   3   4   5   6   1   2   3   4   5   6   1   2   3   4   5   6

SONGS IN 6/8 TIME

"HOUSE OF THE RISING SUN"

This is a good slow song that will give you practice in counting in 6/8 time.
Here are some of the first bars with the counts written under for you to practice.

Notice the pick-up notes and tied notes.
The curved lines between notes on different pitches are "slurs", not ties.

"WHEN JOHNNY COMES MARCHING HOME"

This song has a much faster-moving melody line.
Practice slowly until you can play all the melody notes easily.
Below are some of the first bars with the counts written under for you to practice.
Remember, you do not play the second note of a tie.

STRUMMING CHORDS

Strumming chords to accompany your singing, adds harmony and rhythm to your song.

Your strum arm and wrist should be relaxed and loose, with your forearm moving easily up and down from the elbow and your wrist following with no stiffness or tension.

Where do you strum the strings?
Acoustic guitar - strum over the sound hole.
Electric guitar - strum over the body (not the head).

Strum the strings firmly and evenly, producing a pleasant tone and steady rhythm.

Review pages 32 – 33. Read Chord Symbols and Rhythmic Notation, while strumming down-strokes on each beat.

Using any chords you wish, strum the rhythmic patterns below.

Exercise #1

The note with the square head has the same rhythmic value as a Half Note.

Exercise #2

Exercise #3

Practice all the patterns with the 15 chords in the Instant Chord Chart on page 51. Then, strum the chords to the songs in this book, using these simple down-strokes patterns. Have fun mixing up the patterns and creating your own.

EIGHTH NOTE STRUMMING (with Up-Strokes)

Review page 41, picking eighth notes in a steady rhythm with down-strokes and up-strokes. Pick the down-strokes firmly and the up-strokes more gently.

You can strum chords with an eighth note rhythm using the same technique:
Strum DOWN on the count; and strum UP on the "and". Try it:

Exercise #4

First, without playing, **mime that you're strumming** in an eighth note rhythm, swinging your forearm down and up, keeping a steady rhythm and saying aloud:

" **Down** up **Down** up **Down** up **Down** up "

Keep repeating this mimed rhythm exercise.

Once you have a nice strum rhythm going, substitute counting aloud while miming:

" **1** + **2** + **3** + **4** + "

Repeat this until you feel confident that you can keep your arm swinging in a steady rhythm while you count.

Remember to relax your shoulder and arm, strumming with an easy movement from the elbow and wrist, while you count " **1** + **2** + **3** + **4** + "

Exercise #5

Choose any chord and, with your pick, **strum down and then up** the strings.
Practice slowly, getting a good, full sound on both the down and the up strokes before you concentrate on the rhythm.

When you are ready, add a slow, steady rhythm, saying aloud:

" **Down** up **Down** up **Down** up **Down** up "

Then substitute counts:

" **1** + **2** + **3** + **4** + "

Speed up the rhythm as you gain confidence.

Exercise #6

To add variety and color to your playing, try strumming more forcefully on the down stroke and lightly on the up stroke, saying: " **1 + 2 + 3 + 4** "

Exercise #7

Repeat these techniques with **various chords in 4/4 time**, strumming in eighth notes.

Exercise #8

Practice **different chords in 3/4 time**, strumming in eighth notes.

You will say:

" **Down** up **Down** up **Down** up "

And count: " **1 + 2 + 3 +** "

STRUMMING WITH SONGS

Sing aloud the next three songs - "Jingle Bells", "Twinkle Twinkle Little Star" and "Beautiful Brown Eyes" – strumming an eighth note accompaniment with each song.

Use the rhythmic strumming patterns shown above each song to get you started.

Remember to keep your strumming steady.

Notice that even if the melody of the song has rests or held notes, the **rhythmic strumming pattern stays the same**. For example:

Jin - gle bells	Jin - gle bells	Jin - gle all the	way
⊓ V ⊓ V ⊓ V ⊓ V	⊓ V ⊓ V ⊓ V ⊓ V	⊓ V ⊓ V ⊓ V ⊓ V	⊓ V ⊓ V ⊓ V ⊓ V
1 + 2 + 3 + 4 +	1 + 2 + 3 + 4 +	1 + 2 + 3 + 4 +	1 + 2 + 3 + 4 +

Exercise #9: "Jingle Bells"

Exercise #10: "Twinkle Twinkle"

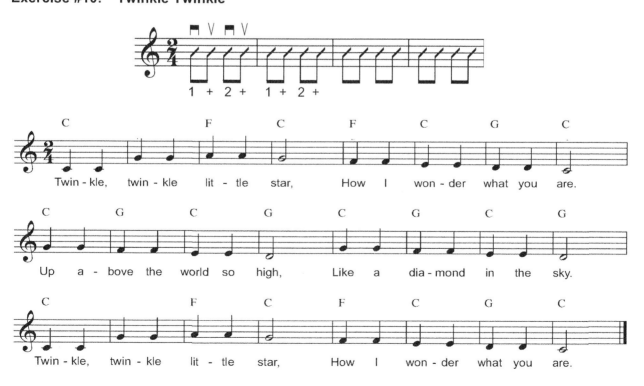

Exercise #11: "Beautiful Brown Eyes"

NEXT STEPS: Keep practicing eighth note strumming to various songs in this book until you feel confident that your strumming sounds full, relaxed and rhythmic.
You can even try making up some patterns of your own. When you listen to your favorite music, see if you can notice the strum patterns and try them yourself.

When you listen to music, you'll notice that in some songs the guitarist, instead of strumming, may pick up and down the chord notes in a rhythmic way, giving a different sound and feeling to the song. You'll learn this "Broken Chord" technique in *Instant Guitar II*.

MORE STRUMMING PATTERNS

To **vary your strumming rhythm**, you can silence some of the strums, adding breaks in the rhythm by **substituting a rest for a strum**.

Here's how: you keep the steady "down-up" rhythm of your arm, but you **don't connect your pick with the strings** on a particular count. That break or silence is shown as a **rest** in rhythmic notation.

Try strumming the patterns, counting and saying the rhythm aloud.

The <u>underlined counts are strummed</u>, the others are silent.

Exercise #12

Say the rhythm aloud first:

"**Down** up **Down** up (*rest*) up **Down** up │ **Down** up **Down** up (*rest*) up **Down** up"

Then count: "**1** + **2** + *3* **+ 4 +** │ **1** + **2** + *3* **+ 4 +**"

Now **mime** strumming in time to your counts before you actually strum the guitar.

1 + 2 + 3 + 4 +

Exercise #13

Say the rhythm aloud first:

"**Down** (*rest*) **Down** up (*rest*) up **Down** up │ **Down** (*rest*) **Down** up (*rest*) up **Down** up"

Then count: "**1** + **2** + *3* **+ 4 +** │ **1** + **2** + *3* **+ 4 +**"

1 + 2 + 3 + 4 +

Exercise #15

Say the rhythm aloud first:

"**Down** (*rest*) **Down** up (*rest*) up **Down** (*rest*) │ **Down** (*rest*) **Down** up (*rest*) up **Down** (*rest*)"

Then count: "**1** + **2+** *3* **+4** + │ **1** + **2+** *3* **+4** +"

1 + 2 + 3 + 4 +

INSTANT CHORD CHART

In this chart you will find all of the chords displayed in this book as well as other common chords you may see in other music you are playing.
Take the time to memorize these 15 chords.

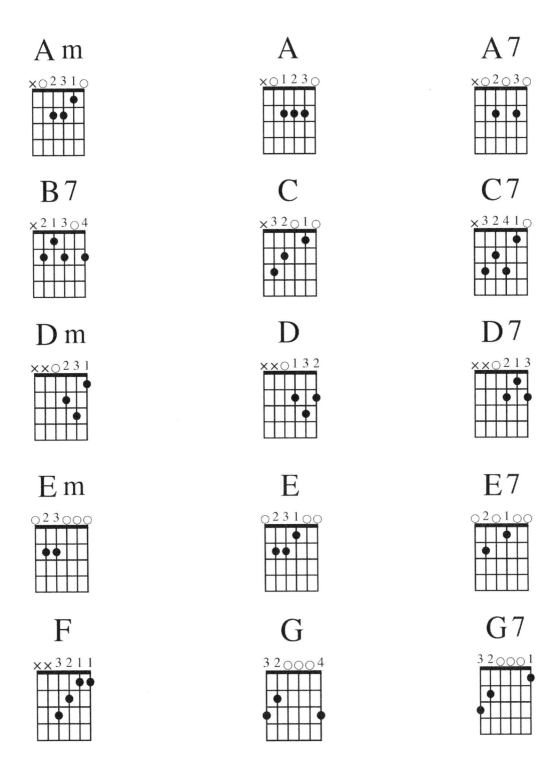

EXTENDED INSTANT CHORD CHART

A **BARRE** above the fingering indicates that **all those strings are pressed down by the same finger**. For example in the Fm chord shown below, the 1st finger is used to press down strings 4, 5 and 6.

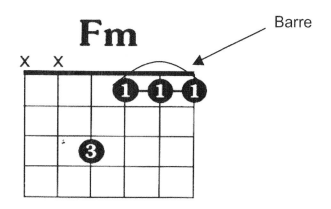

CHORD SYMBOLS

C	= C Major Chord
Cm	= C minor chord
C7	= C Major chord plus the 7th
Cm7	= C minor chord plus the 7th
Cmaj7	= C major chord plus the Major 7th
Cdim or C°	= C diminished chord
C+	= C Augmented Chord
C9	= C chord plus the 9th

Guitar Chord Chart

	C	G	D	A	E	B
Major	C	G	D	A	E	B
Major 6th	C6	G6	D6	A6	E6	B6
Minor	Cm	Gm	Dm	Am	Em	Bm
Minor 6th	Cm6	Gm6	Dm6	Am6	Em6	Bm6
Major 7th	Cmaj7	Gmaj7	Dmaj7	Amaj7	Emaj7	Bmaj7
7th	C7	G7	D7	A7	E7	B7
Minor 7th	Cm7	Gm7	Dm7	Am7	Em7	Bm7
Diminished	Cdim	Gdim	Ddim	Adim	Edim	Bdim
Augmented	C+	G+	D+	A+	E+	B+
9th	C9	G9	D9	A9	E9	B9

X Do not play the string   **O** Play the open string   ① Finger number pressed on string

F B♭(A#) E♭(D#) A♭(G#) D♭(C#) G♭(F#)

	F	**B♭(A#)**	**E♭(D#)**	**A♭(G#)**	**D♭(C#)**	**G♭(F#)**
Major	F	B♭	E♭	A♭	D♭	G♭ (F#)
Major 6th	F6	B♭6	E♭6	A♭6	D♭6	G♭6 (F#6)
Minor	Fm	B♭m	E♭m	A♭m	D♭m	G♭m (F#m)
Minor 6th	Fm6	B♭m6	E♭m6	A♭m6	D♭m6	G♭m6 (F#m6)
Major 7th	Fmaj7	B♭maj7	E♭maj7	A♭maj7	D♭maj7	G♭maj7 (F#maj7)
7th	F7	B♭7	E♭7	A♭7	D♭7	G♭7 (F#7)
Minor 7th	Fm7	B♭m7	E♭m7	A♭m7	D♭m7	G♭m7 (F#m7)
Diminished	Fdim	B♭dim	E♭dim	A♭dim	D♭dim	G♭dim (F#dim)
Augmented	F+	B♭+	E♭+	A♭+	D♭+	G♭+ (F#+)
9th	F9	B♭9	E♭9	A♭9	D♭9	G♭9 (F#9)

X Do not play the string   **O** Play the open string   ① Finger number pressed on string

MORE SONGS TO PRACTICE

"BRAHMS LULLABY"

"SILENT NIGHT"

Si - lent night! Ho - ly night! All is calm,

All is bright. Round yon Vir - gin Moth - er and Child!

Ho - ly In - fant, so ten - der and mild, Sleep in heav - en - ly

peace._____ Sleep____ in heav - en - ly peace._____

"AMAZING GRACE"

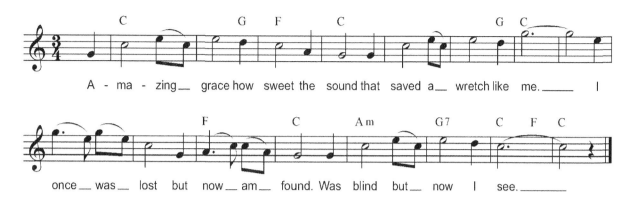

A - ma - zing__ grace how sweet the sound that saved a__ wretch like me.____ I once__ was__ lost but now__ am__ found. Was blind but__ now I see._____

"AMERICA THE BEAUTIFUL"

Oh beau - ti - ful for spa - cious skies for am - ber waves of grain. For pur - ple moun - tain ma - jes - ties a - bove the fruit - ed plain. A - mer - i - ca! A - mer - i - ca! God shed his grace on thee and crown thy good with broth - er - hood from sea to shin - ing sea.

"HAPPY BIRTHDAY"

Notice the 3/4 (waltz) time signature and the pick-up notes

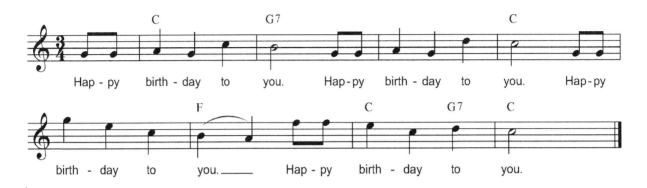

Hap - py birth - day to you. Hap - py birth - day to you. Hap - py

birth - day to you. _____ Hap - py birth - day to you.

"MOZART'S SONATA NO. 15"

This is a great piece to demonstrate chords and scales in a melody.
Notice the accidentals near the end (F# and F natural)

"WE WISH YOU A MERRY CHRISTMAS"

"MY COUNTRY 'TIS OF THEE"

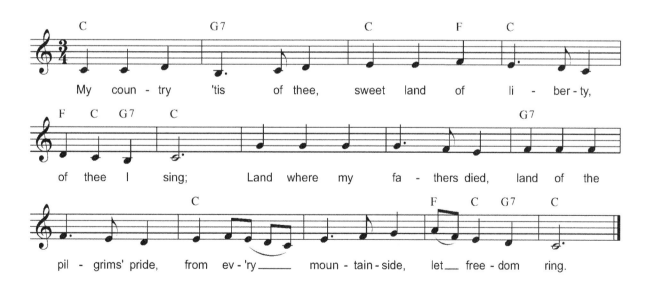

"AURA LEE"

A famous pop song, "Love Me Tender," is based on this melody. Count the dotted
quarter notes carefully "**1** + 2 **+**"

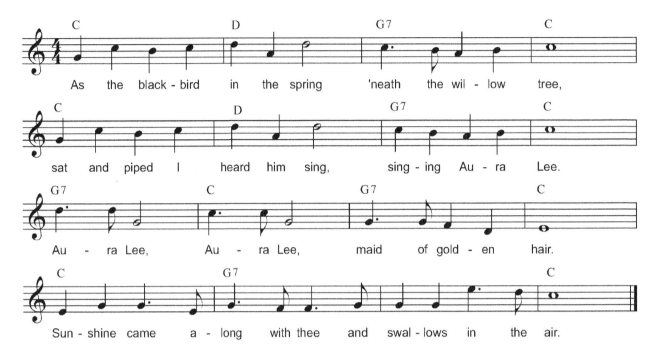

"TENNIS IS A GAME OF LOVE"

This song is available on iTunes.

Music: Charles Segal
Lyrics: Ilonka Bilushka

"YOU'RE NOT ALONE"

Music: Charles Segal
Lyrics: Barbara Brilliant

This song is available on iTunes.

2nd verse:

Somewhere a mother cries
Somewhere a lover weeps
Somewhere a baby fusses
and cannot get to sleep

How does one measure time
It's measured in love not years
Quality's in the giving
The truth is crystal clear

Printed in Great Britain
by Amazon

81095679R00041